FLORIDA

✳ THE DISSTON LANDS. ✳

2,500,000 ACRES,

AT PRICES FROM $1.25 UPWARDS.

OWNED BY THE

Florida Land and Improvement Company.

Atlantic and Gulf Coast Canal and Okeechobee Land Company.

Kissimmee Land Company.

EASY TERMS TO ACTUAL SETTLERS.

Full Information about Florida, Tropical
Fruit Culture, etc.

SOUTH PUBLISHING CO., PRINTERS AND ENGRAVERS, NEW YORK.

FOR FULL DESCRIPTIVE CATALOGUE OF THE LANDS IN EACH COUNTY,
SEND 10 CENTS IN STAMPS TO

✳ FLORIDA LAND AND IMPROVEMENT CO. ✳

305 WALNUT STREET, PHILADELPHIA, PENN.

THE
DISSTON LANDS OF FLORIDA.

OWNED BY THE FOLLOWING COMPANIES:

FLORIDA LAND AND IMPROVEMENT COMPANY.

ATLANTIC AND GULF COAST CANAL AND OKEECHOBEE LAND COMPANY.

KISSIMMEE LAND COMPANY.

2,500,000 ACRES.

AT FROM $1.25 TO $25 PER ACRE. EASY TERMS TO ACTUAL
SETTLERS.

These lands are chiefly in South Florida. They have been carefully selected,
are easy of access by Railroads and Steamers, and are suited for
Winter residences, Tropical fruit and Vegetable culture
and field crops, such as Sugar Cane, Corn,
Rice, Hay, etc. Also large
tracts specially suited
for stock farms
and lumber
mills.

FOR FULL DESCRIPTIVE CATALOGUE SEND 10 CENTS TO

FLORIDA LAND & IMPROVEMENT CO.,

305 WALNUT STREET, PHILADELPHIA, PENN.

1885.

ILLUSTRATED AND PRINTED FOR THE

DISSTON ❋ LAND ❋ COMPANIES,

—BY—

THE SOUTH PUBLISHING COMPANY,

NO. 85 WARREN STREET, NEW YORK.

FLORIDA LAND AND IMPROVEMENT CO.

 Under the Disston purchase this Company in 1881 acquired from the State of Florida the right to select 4,000,000 acres of all the public lands owned by the State. The selection of these was made carefully after thorough inspection during a period of three years, the result being that the lands acquired by this Company were in general the best tracts owned by the State. The title to these lands is indisputable. They were patented by the United States to the State, and conveyed by the State to the Florida Land and Improvement Company, and are free from all debt, mortgage, bond, incumbrance or lien of any character.

LOCATION OF LANDS NOW OWNED BY THIS COMPANY.

		ACRES.			ACRES.
In Duval county,	about	30,000	In Putnam county,	about	2,400
In St. John's county,	"	12,000	In Hernando "	"	206,000
In Volusia "	"	110,000	In Brevard "	"	56,000
In Marion "	"	10,000	In Polk "	"	102,000
In Levy "	"	65,000	In Hillsborough county,	"	161,000
In Alachua "	"	29,000	In Manatee "	"	370,000
In Orange, "	"	61,000	In Monroe "	"	54,000
In Sumter "	"	55,000			

All these lands are within the region of profitable orange culture. Those situated north of Orange, Sumter and Hernando counties are adapted also to cultivation of pears, peaches, grapes, rice, cotton, vegetables of all kinds and ordinary field crops.

In these counties are also good timber tracts and pasture tracts. All of these counties are now accessible by railroads, and many of them by steamers. In Orange, Brevard, Sumter and Hernando counties, besides the products above named, many of the semi-tropical fruits can be grown, with a little sheltering care in winter.

MIDWINTER IN FLORIDA.

Further south are to be found the richest lands in the State, whose soil has no superior in the world. These are the reclaimed lands of the Kissimmee and Caloosahatchee valleys, composed wholly of decomposed vegetable matter, generally from two to ten feet in depth, and underlaid with a sub-soil of calcareous clay or marl. By actual cultivation these lands have produced already, without any fertilizer, the following astonishing yield: Corn, 80 bushels per acre; sugar, 5,000 pounds per acre; rice, 75 bushels per acre; hay, five tons per acre, and vegetables of all kinds in the greatest quantity.

The vegetable grower or truck farmer on these lands can ship to the Northern market without competition from December until May, such shipments including strawberries, tomatoes, potatoes, cucumbers, egg plants, asparagus, cabbages, beets, melons, onions, beans, squashes, etc., and paying him net returns from $200 to $300 per acre.

These reclaimed lands are also the finest stock farms in the world. The native grasses are nutritious, while those who choose can raise choice varieties of forage and pasture grasses on which stock can feed the year round. The water in this region is excellent, and the residence on these lands of Northern people for the last few years has demonstrated beyond all question their entire healthfulness.

The important point of nearest access to these lands is Kissimmee City, on Lake Tohopekaliga, in the southern part of Orange county. This town, only three years old has a population of about 1,200, with several hotels, churches, schools, excellent stores, and bids fair to become one of the largest cities in Florida. No tourist or prospective settler should visit Florida without going to Kissimmee City and taking a trip down the Kissimmee valley, through its beautiful lakes and rivers, and stopping at Southport farm, fourteen miles below Kissimmee, to inspect these rich lands and the crops growing upon them.

Besides these reclaimed lands, we have in this southern range of counties many hundred thousand acres of pine, prairie and hammock lands extending from the counties of Orange, Sumter and Hernando, southward past Tampa Bay and Charlotte Harbor, as far as Cape Romano on the Gulf. Many of these lands are suited to tropical fruit culture; others are better suited to the culture of vegetables, rice, corn, hay and all products requiring moist, rich soil.

In these southern counties are the finest pasturage lands in the State, and here we can sell excellent stock farms of any desired size from 5,000 to 100,000 acres.

By sending ten cents in postage stamps to the Land Commissioner of this Company at Jacksonville, Florida, a complete descriptive catalogue of its lands can be obtained.

The minimum price for lands of this Company is $1.25 per acre; from that they range upwards according to location and quality, choice sugar lands being worth $25 per acre.

VIEW IN J. A. HARRIS GROVE, CITRA, FLA.

ATLANTIC AND GULF COAST CANAL AND OKEECHOBEE LAND COMPANY.

(COMMONLY KNOWN AS THE OKEECHOBEE DRAINAGE COMPANY.)

Early in 1881 this Company was organized by Hamilton Disston and his associates under a special charter obtained from the Legislature of the State of Florida, and under a contract between the Company and the Board of Trustees of Internal Improvements of the State of Florida, authorized by acts of the United States Congress, and of the Legislature of Florida, it at once commenced operations.

Its charter and contracts provided that the Company should undertake and prosecute the drainage and reclamation of more than 8,000,000 acres, being about one-fourth of the State lying south of Orange county and east of Peace creek. This field of operations includes both the Kissimmee and Caloosahatchee valleys, the region around Lake Okeechobee, and the large area known as the Everglades extending southward from Lake Okeechobee to Cape Sable, and lies almost wholly within the counties of Polk, Manatee, Brevard, Monroe and Dade. The Company acquires one-half of the lands.

Within a few months after the organization of the Company its first powerful dredge was built and commenced cutting a canal from the Caloosahatchee river to Lake Okeechobee. This canal was finished in 1882, and ever since then the w ters of Lake Okeechobee have for the first time within the knowledge of man flowed constantly to the Gulf, lowering the lake level and preventing a recurrence of the former annual verflow of the rich lands on the upper Caloosahatchee and the borders of Okeechobee.

In December, 1881, the Okeechobee Drainage Company commenced work at the northern limit of their territory. In that m nth they cut the first tree and built the first house where Kissimmee City now stands, and established there their shops and boat yard for the construction of dredges and steamers. At this point three additional dredges have successively been built and put into operation cutting drainage canals. One of these dredges alone has an excavating capacity equal to that of 2,500 men with shovels.

Working southward from Kissimmee City, these dredges have cut many canals and straightened and widened rivers and creeks, reclaiming hundreds of thousands of acres of the richest land on earth, whose quality and value have been described above.

A FLORIDA AVENUE.

LANDS NOW OWNED BY THE OKEECHOBEE COMPANY.

At the present time this Company owns about 1,200,000 acres in the counties of Brevard, Polk, Manatee and Monroe. Their title to these lands is clear, being the same as to those of the Florida Land and Improvement Company. They are classified as sugar lands, pine lands and prairie lands.

The sugar lands are the rich reclaimed lands described above, being generally along the lakes, canals and water courses.

The pine lands are of the same general class as described elsewhere, and are suited to fruit and vegetable culture and general settlement, as well as for pasture.

The prairie lands are generally best suited for pasturage. Those of them lying near the sugar lands are especially adapted for gardening and general farming.

A descriptive catalogue of the lands owned by this Company will be found in the same pamphlet with those of the Florida Land and Improvement Company.

The minimum price of its lands is $1.25 per acre; from that upwards to $25 per acre for best sugar lands.

KISSIMMEE LAND COMPANY.

This Company was incorporated and organized in 1883 under the general Incorporation Act of Florida, by some of the prominent men of the Florida

LAKE WYOMI, FLA.

Land and Improvement Company, and other capitalists interested in the settlement of Florida. Its purpose was to acquire the ownership of a limited quantity of choice, carefully selected tracts of land, which are offered for sale chiefly to actual settlers. This Company owns the following properties:

KISSIMMEE CITY:

One-half of the business lots in the original plat of this town; also 480 acres (being its addition to Kissimmee), divided into five-acre lots. The busi-

AN ORANGE NURSERY.

ness lots in the center of the town are sold at from $200 to $600 per lot, according to location; the five-acre lots at from $300 to $500 per lot. These are well suited for residence, groves and gardens.

RURAL PROPERTY.

	ACRES.			ACRES.
In Sumter county,	about 4,000	In Hernando county,	about	3,000
In Orange "	" 10,000	In Brevard "	"	6,000
In Polk "	" 15,500	In Manatee "	"	35,500
In Hillsborough county,	" 14,000	In Monroe "	"	22,500

The minimum price for the pine lands of this Company is $2.50 per acre; from that figure prices range upwards to $5, and for a few choice locations as high as $10..

A FLORIDA MAMMOTH TREE.

GENERAL INFORMATION ABOUT FLORIDA.

HISTORICAL.

Florida was discovered in 1497 by Sebastian Cabot; permanently settled in 1565; ceded to Great Britain in 1763, with a population of only six hundred; after a colonial existence of two hundred years, receded to Spain in 1784; sold and ceded to the United States in 1819; harassed and plundered by repeated Indian wars from 1816 t. 1858, receiving a territorial government in 1822; admitted to the Union in 1845, seceding in 1861 and reconstructed in 1868; and since 1874 has, in a small measure, commenced to receive that attention from settlers which its climate, soil and natural resources call for.

TOPOGRAPHICAL.

This, the most southern of all the states, is a peninsula projecting down between the Atlantic ocean and Gulf of Mexico. Its area comprises nearly 60,000 square miles, or 35,000,000 acres. Its peculiar position, its peninsular form, its ocean and Gulf surroundings, make it exceptional, and unlike any other country lying in the same latitude. The truly peninsular portion of Florida is some 300 miles in length, and averages about 100 miles in width, gradually narrowing from north to south. The nearness of that great ocean river, the Gulf Stream, to its shores, causes the trade winds of the Atlantic to sweep over the land from east to west by day, the returning cool winds from the Gulf gently blowing across the State by night. The stranger is incredulous of the peculiar temperature, until, by sojourning here, he finds, although the day be warm, the succeeding night is invariably cool. These daily constant breezes purify and vivify the atmosphere, and preserve it from stagnation or sultriness.

About midway from north to south, the lands bordering on the ocean and Gulf are more or less level, broken by occasional ridges reaching 180 feet in height. In East Florida, about half way from the sea to the Suwannee river, there is a table-land elevation which extends south nearly to the Everglades. The extreme southern portion of the State is low, though from recent surveys it is found that it can be effectually drained and made available for cultivation. No State in the Union has such an extent of coast, being nearly 1,200 miles in length, indented every few miles by large bays, running inland in many places from ten to thirty miles, with large rivers like the St. Johns, St. Marys,

Suwannee, Ocklawaha, Withlacoochee, Kissimmee, Caloosahatchee, and Peace creek, navigable for great distances. There are other connecting navigable streams in all parts of the State, and lakes, large and small, scattered and grouped together, all of which abound in excellent varieties of fish, and furnish local transportation facilities; many connect with navigable streams, and all can be easily connected by short canals or railroads with each other and the great arteries of water leading to the sea and Gulf. The interior lakes of Florida, large and small, are among its remarkable features.

The soil in the greater portion of the State is a sandy loam, except in the lowlands and hammocks, where large portions of clay and alluvium are found. The soil d_es not resemble the sandy lands of other states; it has more or less of loam and a large percentage of lime and organic remains, giving it much fertility. The country is well watered, not only by its larger and smaller rivers and lakes, but by innumerable creeks and springs. Springs of great volume are found in every portion of the State, some of such magnitude that they form navigable rivers from their source; of such are the Blue Springs, in Jackson county, in the west; Wakulla Springs, in Wakulla county, in the middle; Silver Springs, in Marion county, in the east; the very large Blue Spring on the St. Johns, in Volusia county; the Green Cove Spring, in Clay county, on the shore of the St. Johns; also Clay Spring, in Orange county. Some of these are medicinal—white sulphur, iron, etc. Good water, so universally desired, is found easily at a depth of from eight to fifty feet, according to locality—generally from twelve to twenty feet; but, through the country, the many lakes and springs and branches afford ample supply for house and farm purposes. An ordinary gas pipe of one and a half or two inches in diameter, shod with a conical plug of iron, and perforated for a distance of one or two feet above the plug, will, when driven into the ground to a depth of thirty to forty-five feet, afford a never-failing flow of water, at all times cool and refreshing; the flow is, in many cases, so strong that faucets are placed on the pipe from thirty inches to three feet above the ground in order to check it. Artesian wells give an enormous flow of pure water at a depth of 200 to 300 feet.

POLITICAL.

The present Constitution of Florida was adopted in 1868. It is similar to the later constitutions of the North and West, somewhat modified, being more liberal in suffrage and exemption clauses. No county can have more than four Assemblymen; every county can have *one*. Foreigners who may become residents enjoy the same rights as to property as native-born citizens. The Legislature consists of a Senate and Assembly, the first elected for four years, the latter for two years, biennial sessions. All property of wife, owned before or acquired after marriage, is made separate, and not liable to debts of the husband. The Governor is elected for four years; he appoints all officials, the most important with consent of the Senate, except constables, who are elected.

There are the usual Cabinet, Supreme Court, Circuit Courts, County Judges and Justices of the Peace. There is a school system similar to that of the North, which makes provision for free schools for all children. The school fund consists of proceeds of all United States lands granted for educational purposes, the Agricultural College fund donated by the Government, and fines under penal laws; also a special State tax of *one mill* on all taxable property, annually levied; and each county is permitted to levy not exceeding four mills for county school purposes.

CLIMATE.

The climate of Florida is so well known throughout the civilized world that it is not necessary to go into detail; we will briefly give some facts from official tables, and the opinions of scientists. It is *not* a *hot* climate in summer, but mild, and not subject to great changes of temperature. The winters are not *cold* and *freezing*, but uniformly *cool* and *pleasant*. Throughout the whole twelve months, the rainy, cloudy, disagreeable days are the exception; fair, bright, sunny days the rule. The thermometer seldom goes below 30 deg. in winter, and rarely above 90 deg in summer. The official records show the daily average for summer, 78 deg.; for winter, 60 deg. The daily constant ocean breezes in summer modify the heat (the Gulf breeze, coming with the setting sun, cools the air at night); a warm or sultry night is almost unknown. Official sanitary reports, both of scientific bodies and the army, show that Florida stands first in health, although in the reports are included the transient or recent population, many of whom take refuge here as invalids, some in the lowest stages of disease. In the middle and southern portions of the State frost is rarely known. The summer is longer, but the heat less oppressive than midsummer at the North; this results from its peculiar peninsular shape and the constant breezes which pass over the State. For days together, New York, Boston and Chicago show, in summer, temperature as high as 100 deg.; it is very rare that it reaches that degree in Florida for a single day, generally ranging below 90 deg.; not oppressive, modified by the ever-changing air; not sultry, close or humid; mornings and evenings always cool. Natives and old residents, if asked, would say they preferred the summer to the winter months for climate.

We take from Dr. A. S. Baldwin's tables, kept for the Smithsonian Institute, as follows:

Jacksonville, latitude 30 deg. 15 min., longitude 82 deg.—mean of three daily observations for twenty years—1844–1867. Thermometer:

January,	55 deg.	May,	76 deg.	September,	78 deg.
February,	58 "	June,	80 "	October,	70 "
March,	64 "	July,	82 "	November,	62 "
April,	70 "	August,	82 "	December,	52 "

The Army records show for twenty years, variation at St. Augustine, Fla., 23 degrees.

LAKE CONWAY, FLA.

Rainfall at Jacksonville, average for ten years, 54.5 inches; the largest quantity in August and September, and the least in November.

Another important question both for comfort and health is *relative humidity*, and here Florida stands, strange to say, ahead of all other states for the dryness of its atmosphere.

FROM UNITED STATES SIGNAL SERVICE REPORTS DURING A SERIES OF YEARS.	Jacksonville.	St. Paul, Minnesota.	Atlantic City, New Jersey.	Nassau, Bahama Islands.
Mean humidity for five winter months, from 1875 to 1880, . . .	69 deg.	71.3 deg.	78.1 deg.	73.2 deg.
Mean humidity for the month of March, 1875 to 1880, ...	63.9 deg.	67.1 deg.	76.8 deg.	68.4 deg.

SOCIETY.

All classes are found, as in other states, and the questions of nativity, antecedents and political or religious views create as few distinctions as can probably be found in any community in the world.

The stranger is welcomed, and the new comer finds friendly neighbors around him. Within the last ten years thousands of Northern people have settled in Florida, and engaged in fruit and vegetable growing, as well as other business and professional occupations. This large, new element is regarded and treated by native Floridians as most welcome and desirable, and the State authorities and private citizens join in making their coming pleasant and their residence satisfactory.

The section of the State in which most of the land of these Companies has been selected is the favored location for orange groves and the growing of fruits and vegetables for Northern markets. The aggregate population of Orange, Sumter, Hernando, Hillsborough, Polk and Manatee counties, in 1880, was 29,234; in 1885, it is 52,000. Only 3,741 of this number were colored—a fair guarantee that throughout this region the white population and white labor will always be in the ascendency. In the cotton region of the northern part of the State, the colored outnumber the white citizens.

HOMESTEAD AND OTHER EXEMPTIONS.

One hundred and sixty acres, or one-half acre of land within city or town, owned by the head of a family residing in the State, together with one thousand dollars of personal property, and the improvements on the real estate, shall be exempted from any forced sale under any process of law; and real estate shall not be alienable without the joint written consent of wife and husband.

STATE AND COUNTY TAXES.

The State levies, annually, one mill tax for school purposes. For the current year (1885) four mills are levied for expenses of State government and interest on bonded debt; total State tax, five mills. Counties must levy one-half mill for school purposes, and not exceeding four mills for county purposes; total, nine and one half mills, or less than one per cent. of the assessed value of the property.

INSTRUCTIONS FOR SETTLERS.

These Companies offer their lands at cheap rates, and on favorable terms of payment, to encourage a rapid settlement of the same by citizens of all countries skilled in farming, gardening, fruit growing, cultivation of tobacco, sugar, grapes, oranges, and the raising of cattle, etc. We invite specially those having sufficient capital and energy to become land-owners, permanent residents and successful agriculturists; and to become such, every settler should have at least $500 to $800 on arriving in Florida. This amount will secure land, and such farming implements as are required.

If you settle on cleared land, you can at once plant vegetables that will give you a return in from three to five months. On the lands of these Companies you can raise fruits and vegetables *every month* in the year, though, of course, certain seasons are best adapted to certain crops.

HOW TO GET THERE.

From New York, Philadelphia and Baltimore there are regular steamers to Jacksonville, Fernandina and Savannah, from which points the lands of these Companies can be easily and cheaply reached by water or rail.

Regular steamer rates from New York or Philadelphia to Jacksonville are, including meals, first-class, $25; emigrant, $13.

From all Northern cities there are through routes by railroad to Jacksonville and other points in Florida, with parlor and sleeping-cars and fast freight lines.

Present regular rates by railroad are about as follows:

				First-class.
From Boston	to Jacksonville,	. . . .	$37 30
" New York	" "	.	31 00
" Philadelphia	" "	. . .	28 56
" Baltimore	" "	. . .	25 70
" Richmond	" "	. . ,	22 50
" Cincinnati	" "	. . .	22 75
" Chicago	" "	. . .	29 75
" St. Louis	" "	. . , .	27 35
" St. Paul	" "	. . . .	42 25

The time from New York to Jacksonville by rail is now reduced to forty-six hours. From Philadelphia to Jacksonville, forty-three hours.

HOUSEHOLD EXPENSES.

A VERY IMPORTANT ITEM.

Regular steamer and rail freights from New York to Jacksonville (and all other points in Florida) are not high, as will appear from the following list of leading articles:

Flour, per bbl., ... $0 35	Furniture, per cwt., ... $0 40
Bacon, per cwt., ... 28	Agricultural Imp., per cwt., . 1 15
Boxed goods, per cwt., . . . 40	General Groceries, " . 50

By sailing vessels rates are about half as much.

Groceries, dry goods, hardware, etc., can be bought from the Florida merchants as cheaply on the average as in any Northern State, and it is not necessary to bring any large supply, if the settler has money to buy what he needs after reaching his new home.

At Jacksonville prices are about as follows:

Flour, per bbl, . . . $4 00 to $6 50	Butter, per lb., . . . $0 25 to $0 40
Bacon, per cwt., . . 6 50 to 7 00	Coffee, " . . . 19 to 30
Sugar, per lb., ... 06 to 08	and other articles in proportion.

WAGES AND OTHER EXPENSES.

For house servants, $5 to $8 per month; farm laborers, $15 to $20 and rations (costing $6 per month); day laborers, 50 cents and $1 per diem; common mechanics, $1 to $1.25; skilled labor higher and in demand.

Fuel (wood) is cheap, generally to be had for cutting and hauling, and seldom needed except for cooking.

Horses and mules cost from $50 to $150; carts, $25 to $30; plows, such as generally used, $3 to $6. All needed agricultural implements can be bought cheaper in Florida than to buy them North and pay freight on them.

SOIL.

The so-called sand of Florida is not the sharp silicious sand of the ocean-washed beach, or the fine inorganic sand which forms the pine barrens of the North and West. Composed, in great part, of a mixture of humus, lime and loam, the surface sand of Florida has good fertilizing qualities. Florida lands are ordinarily classified as pine lands, hammocks (lands covered with hard woods), and prairie lands. The greater portion of the State is covered with pine—the pitch and yellow pine. The hammocks, high and low, are densely covered with hard wood, such as live oak, oak, magnolia, gum, hickory, etc. The prairie lands are some of them extremely rich. The first-rate pine lands, so called, are generally elevated and rolling, covered with a dark vegetable mould or humus several inches deep, resting on a chocolate-colored sandy loam, mixed with pebble and lime; under this, clay and soft limestone rock. These lands have a durable fertility, and are well adapted to the usual agricultural products and semi-tropical fruits. They are found to withstand drought well, and in rainy seasons growing crops are not affected except favorably. They are healthy, the water is pure, and it costs little to prepare the soil for cultivation. It is noticeable that the early settlers selected these lands especially for residences and home farms, health, pure water, freedom from insects, good soil for crops and fruit, and ease of cultivation. They produce well for years without fertilizing, but readily respond in increased products to fertilizers. The second rate pine lands, which are also timbered with pine, are more or less high and rolling, are well watered, the surface soil is not deep, are underlaid with clay or limestone, and produce well for a few years; fertilized, they yield good crops of cotton, corn, cane and root crops; when properly cultivated, they are superior for semi-tropical fruits. Experienced growers have selected this class of land for orange groves.

COST OF CLEARING LAND.

The cost of clearing land depends on whether sparsely timbered or of thick growth; whether pine, hammock or swamp land, and also whether the land is to be planted in orange groves or usual crops. It was formerly the custom to simply girdle the trees and ran ove the fallen timber. This was done quickly and cheaply, and crops put in the same season.

To clear ordinary pine land, removing the timber, will cost from $12 to $15 per acre; hammock lands will cost more—from $25 to $40, according to the density and size of timber.

For a new place, the Virginia rail fence is cheapest, as timber is on the spot, and splits freely. There are saw-mills throughout the Disston purchase, so that boards and posts may be substituted.

COST OF BUILDING.

The new-comer, anxious to have a roof over his head and be ready to go to work, will hasten to build him a house. Now, here is room and range for any person to exercise his taste, talent, extravagance or economy. A comfortable log-house for a moderate-sized family can be built, say, for $50; a good frame building, with four or five rooms, will cost from $200 to $500. Lumber of fair quality, generally $12 per 1,000 feet, at mills.

Any one moving his family to a new State should have either money or provisions to last until he can raise crops.

EARLY VEGETABLES FOR NORTHERN MARKETS.

The raising of these is now, and always will be, extremely profitable in Florida, and the farther south the greater the profit. The business in this State began in a small way near Fernandina and Jacksonville ten years ago, and has greatly increased; but there is an enormous field for expansion, and the subject is worthy the special attention of settlers.

Their crops of early vegetables bring them quick cash returns within from four to five months after planting, at high prices, the yield of a single acre often reaching from $100 to $400. The principal vegetables shipped north from Florida are potatoes, tomatoes, egg plant, cucumbers, watermelons, cabbage and strawberries. Onions should be largely raised, and would be among the most profitable.

The early supplies for the North come at present from the following sources: South Florida, in January and February; Bermuda, commencing in March; Northern Florida, about the same date as Bermuda; Savannah and Charleston, three to four weeks later than Florida; Norfolk, ten days' later than Charleston. Then prices fall, and Maryland and New Jersey follow in quick succession.

Florida holds the key of the most valuable part of this trade. Settlers on the lands of these Companies can entirely supplant Bermuda in the trade, being four to eight weeks ahead of Northern Florida, which has already taken the cream from Charleston, and rendered the immense "truck" farms around Norfolk unprofitable. For two or three months Florida can have this trade all to herself, at the highest prices.

The following quotations given by WARRINGTON, MATLACK & Co., Commission Merchants, Philadelphia, present a comparison of the prices obtained for four kinds of early produce from the four leading sources of supply, for the season of 1881:

	POTATOES. Per Barrel.			TOMATOES. Per 3-peck Crate. (¾-Bushel.)			ASPARAGUS. Per Bunch.			STRAWBERRIES. Per Quart.		
	Commencement of Season.	End of Season.	Average for entire Crop.	Commencement of Season.	End of Season.	Average for entire Crop.	Commencement of Season.	End of Season.	Average for entire Crop.	Commencement of Season.	End of Season.	Average for entire Crop.
Bermuda....	$12 00	7 00	8 00	In small boxes at very high prices.			None raised.			None raised.		
N'th Florida	8 00	4 00	5 00	5 00	2 00	2 50	1 00	50	75	1 00	75	80
Charleston..	6 00	2 00	4 00	2.00	75	1 00	75	25	50	60	25	35
Norfolk	4 00	1 50	2 00	2 50	30	75	75	10	25	25	05	08

Prices for South Florida produce are higher than Bermuda.

The first Florida strawberries bring from $3 to $4 per quart.

NOTE.—Vegetable crops on the lands of these Companies, in Middle and South Florida, mature from three to four weeks earlier than those in North Florida.

Settlers on the lands of these Companies will have quick transit North for their produce, and by planting in the fall and winter, can have the early market to themselves at high prices. These crops will supply the home table, and put a nice sum in the grower's pocket, while other crops are maturing.

HOW TO MAKE AN ORANGE GROVE.

The judicious selection of the land is the first and most important point, for on this, success in a great measure depends. Choose dry hammock, or pine land that has natural drainage. The most favorable locations in North Florida are on the southeast side of wide sheets of water, or high lands, which are more generally free from frost. In South Florida this is not important. The land selected, clear thoroughly of all trees, etc., break up well, and substantially fence; sow with cow peas, which turn under when in bloom, it improves and sweetens the soil; this may be done before or after planting trees. Dig holes thirty feet apart, eighteen inches deep and four feet in diameter, clean out all roots, fill up with top soil, which will retain the moisture, procure trees from three to five years old, take them up carefully, with all of the roots possible, pack up with wet moss as soon as dug, put in shade and out of the wind, take to the proposed grove carefully, remove soil from holes dug sufficient for the tree, with roots carefully spread, trunk standing in same position as originally grown. Let the tree, when set out, be fully an inch above the natural level of the land; fill under, in and about the roots, compactly—it is best done by the hand, filled to the surface and gently tramped down; fill on some two or three inches of earth, which will prevent drying; the rainy season commencing, remove the soil about the tree to the level about it. Cultivation should be frequent and shallow, and trash not allowed to accumulate near trunk; light plowing and raking near the trees is best and safest. Following these general directions, no one should fail. The cost of a five-acre grove, at, say, five years from planting, at a liberal estimate where high pine land is chosen, will be about as given below. If hammock land is taken, the cost of clearing will be more. The grove will have begun to yield at the end of the period named. Rev. T. E. Moore, Fruit Cove, Fla., has published a good treatise on orange culture.

COST OF GROVE.

Five acres of good land, variously estimated, depending on location.

Cutting timber, clearing, ...	$ 75 00
Fencing (post and board fence), and breaking up, ...	75 00
Three hundred trees, and setting out, ...	200 00
Manures, labor, cultivating, taxes, etc., for five years, . . .	500 00
Total, less cost of land, ...	$850 00

Such a grove would readily sell now in Florida for $1,000 per acre. From and after five years the annual growth of trees and increase of fruit is constant, and thereafter the grove will hold its vigor and fruit-producing qualities for a century or more. The orange is a hardy tree, will stand great extremes of rain and drought; it will show the effects of a single season's neglect, and quickly show a single season of care and attention.

The general varieties of the orange are the sour, the sweet, and the bitter-sweet. The sour and bitter-sweet are supposed to be indigenous, growing wild in the forests. The orange, as also all of the same family, can be grown from the seed, grafting, budding, and cuttings. All are rapid in growth, annual and abundant bearers, long-lived, easily cultivated, hardy, and not as subject to disease or destruction as most trees. Budded, the sweet orange will commence to bear the third year; the seedling in the sixth year, increasing each succeeding year; at fifteen to twenty years averaging at least 5,000 each.

WHEN AND WHAT TO PLANT.

These directions are for the latitude of Jacksonville. The lands of these Companies are from four to eight weeks earlier in planting and maturing crops, and hot-beds are not needed.

In JANUARY, plant Irish potatoes, peas, beets, turnips, cabbage, and all hardy or semi-hardy vegetables; make hot-beds for pushing the more tender plants, such as melons, tomatoes, okra, egg-plants, etc.; set out fruit and other trees, and shrubbery.

FEBRUARY—Keep planting for a succession, same as in January; in addition, plant vines of all kinds, shrubbery, and fruit trees of all kinds, especially of the citrus family, snap beans, corn; bed sweet potatoes for draws and slips. Oats may also be still sown, as they are in previous months.

MARCH—Corn, oats, and planting of February may be continued; transplant tomatoes, egg-plants, melons, beans, and vines of all kinds; mulberries and blackberries are now ripening.

APRIL—Plant as in March, except Irish potatoes, kohl rabi, turnips; continue to transplant tomatoes, okra, egg-plants; sow millet, corn, cow peas, for fodder; plant the butter bean, lady peas; dig Irish potatoes. Onions, beets and usual early vegetables should be plenty for table.

MAY—Plant sweet potatoes for draws in beds; continue planting corn for table; snap beans, peas and cucumbers ought to be well forward for use; continue planting okra, egg-plants, pepper, and butter beans.

JUNE—The heavy planting of sweet potatoes and cow peas is now in order; Irish potatoes, tomatoes, and a great variety of table vegetables are now ready, as also plums, early peaches and grapes.

JULY—Sweet potatoes and cow peas are safe to plant, the rainy season being favorable; grapes, peaches and figs are in full season. Orange trees may be set out if the season is wet.

AUGUST—Finish up planting sweet potatoes and cow peas; sow cabbage, cauliflower, turnips for fall planting; plant kohl rabi and rutabagas; transplant orange trees and bud; last of month plant a few Irish potatoes and beans.

SEPTEMBER—Now is the time to commence for the true winter garden, the garden which is commenced in the North in April and May. Plant the whole range of vegetables except sweet potatoes; set out asparagus, onion sets and strawberry plants.

OCTOBER—Plant same as last month; put in garden peas; set out cabbage plants; dig sweet potatoes, sow oats, rye, etc.

NOVEMBER—A good month for garden; continue to plant and transplant, same as for October; sow oats, barley and rye for winter pasturage crops; dig sweet potatoes, house or bank them; make sugar and syrup.

DECEMBER—Clear up generally; fence, ditch, manure, and sow and plant hardy vegetables; plant, set out orange trees, fruit trees and shrubbery; keep a sharp look-out for an occasional frost; a slight protection will prevent injury.

The settler of limited means needs but little land. From five to forty acres, well selected, are enough for him. He can plant sugar cane, that will pay handsomely every year. He can set out his orange grove at once, and at the same time plant crops that will support his family and pay him some cash besides within the first eight months. He can plant also, if he settles far enough south, bananas and pineapples that will pay very large returns within from eight to fourteen months.

PRODUCTIONS.

The lands of these Companies produce nearly all the crops and fruits of the Middle, Northern and Southern States, and, in addition, a great variety of semi-tropical and tropical fruits and vegetables, and most of the best known and valuable medicinal and fibrous plants.

CORN.

Corn, which is the great staple raised in the United States, especially in the West, and which exceeds by many millions of bushels any and all other crops, is grown in all portions of the State; and the produce per acre is here, as elsewhere, more or less, according to fertility of soil and cultivation. Good hammock or pine land will produce twenty to twenty-five bushels, and on our rich reclaimed lands from 75 to 100 bushels per acre are produced.

One person with one horse or mule can easily cultivate from thirty to forty acres; and as the time for growing a crop of corn is from four to five months, it leaves ample time to cultivate another crop of peas or sweet potatoes, with same labor on same land. The corn usually raised is the white variety, largely used in meal and hominy for food, especially at the South.

WHEAT, RYE, OATS.

Wheat in the northern section of the State can be grown, but is not raised as a regular crop. Rye and oats do well, and are mostly sown early in the fall, affording a good winter pasturage; mature in early spring, and are not threshed, being cured and fed to stock in the straw.

RICE.

There are thousands of acres in every section of the State peculiarly adapted to the successful culture of rice. Its cultivation is as simple as that of any cereal; usually drilled and kept clear of weeds; twenty-five to seventy-five bushels of rough rice per acre is a fair crop. Recent introduction of improved rice machinery, adapted for individual or neighborhood use, will stimulate increased production.

This crop will be very profitable on our reclaimed lands.

TOBACCO.

Tobacco will grow anywhere in the State. A superior quality of Cuba tobacco, from imported seed, is grown in Gadsden and adjoining counties, and fully equals the best imported. Before the war it was extensively and profitably cultivated, and mostly sold to Germany, agents visiting the State to purchase. It requires careful attention, will yield from 500 to 700 pounds to the acre, and sells for from twenty to thirty cents per pound. Latterly there is an increasing home and State demand by cigar manufacturers, and the area of cultivation is extending.

SWEET POTATOES.

White or black, no family is so poor as to be without a potato patch. It yields all the way from 100 to 400 bushels to the acre, according to soil, cultivation and season; is grown from roots, draws and slips; planted from April to August, maturing from July to November; is of easy cultivation, and may be dug, safely banked in field and yard, or housed. There are many varieties planted, good and indifferent, and there is no excuse for not raising the best.

THE CITRUS FAMILY.

This includes the orange, lemon, lime, grape fruit, shaddock, citron and similar fruits; there are several varieties of each, and new varieties are produced from time to time, as with other fruits. Under modern culture, superior size, flavor and color are obtained. The lemon is more prolific than the orange, bearing earlier; the lime still more than the lemon; both, however, are more sensitive to frost, and cannot be generally grown north of the land of these Companies. The grape fruit and shaddock are similar in shape to the orange, though larger, and have a sub-acid flavor; they are not grown for extensive sale, yet many persons like the taste. The citron is of two varieties—the ordinary smooth skinned and the ribbed kind; both grow to a large size, the latter being the species of commerce.

SUGAR CANE.

Fair land will produce from 1,500 to 2,000 pounds of sugar per acre; our reclaimed lands will produce from 3,000 to 5,000 pounds. Recent improvements in sugar machinery have obviated the necessity of expensive works formerly required, rendering it possible for the small as well as the large planter to manufacture cheaply, as its cultivation is as easy as corn, and its immunity from all hurt by ordinary enemies to other vegetation, renders it a safe crop. In Louisiana the yield, owing to the shorter season, etc., is only 800 to 1,500 pounds per acre.

BANANA, PINEAPPLE, ETC.

In Southern Florida, the pineapple and banana are successfully grown; the fruit is of a finer quality, and larger size, than most imported from abroad. The banana plant is simply planted and let alone, maturing its fruit in from fifteen to eighteen months; shedding its large leaves, it dies down, and sends up suckers at its base, a single one of which perpetuates the old stock. The others may be replanted in new places.

The pineapple is planted from the suckers or shoots of the matured fruit and main stock. The guava, of which there are several varieties in size, color and taste, is a rapid grower and an abundant bearer. It fruits in two years from seed, is delicious as a table fruit when ripe, and makes a superior marmalade, jelly and preserves.

MELONS.

The Northern man who has only seen the prize melon, pumpkin, squash, and other fruits of similar kind, is astounded at the size of Florida growth. It is no rare thing to see watermelons three feet long, weighing seventy pounds, muskmelons twenty to thirty pounds, and pumpkins and squashes will often weigh a hundred pounds. Muskmelons also are of large size, and delicious cantaloupes are raised easily; indeed, vines of all kinds succeed well, the long, warm season favoring rapid growth.

STRAWBERRIES.

This queen of small fruits nowhere in the world finds a better location for culture; plants put out in September fruit often in January, frequently in February, and may be counted in full bearing and ripening in March and April. The growers about Jacksonville and up the St. Johns river are many, and shipments have been made largely and profitably. In size, color, bouquet and taste they are unsurpassed, the best varieties only being grown. The cultivators pick carefully, select and pack honestly; and Florida strawberries, like Florida oranges, have earned a name. By using refrigerators the fruit reaches New York and Northern cities fresh and cool, only about four days from picking, bringing extravagant prices, the first shipments bringing from $3 to $5 per quart.

APPLES, PEARS, QUINCES AND PEACHES.

Apples are of the early varieties, ripening in May and June. Pears do well. We have seen some grown here fully equal in size and flavor to the California product. The quince attains the size of a standard apple tree; fruit large, but flavor not as pronounced as at the North.

The peach is a sure tree here, bearing in two years from the graft, and early varieties of good size and flavor ripening in May, June and July. The apricot and nectarine are also safe to cultivate.

GRAPES, PLUMS AND CHERRIES.

Most of the American and foreign varieties of grape are easily grown, ripening from June to November. The St. Augustine grape, so called, is a choice grape for eating or wine. The Scuppernong in all its varieties is cultivated largely, being a rapid grower, an abundant bearer, long-lived, and needing but little pruning or care.

Plums are found growing wild all over the State, many of good size and flavor; where cultivated are much improved. The black cherry is also found

LAKE WEIR, FLA.

wild, but the tame or cultivated cherry does not seem to succeed, though we see no reason why it should not, when fruits of similar habit grow well.

PEANUTS.

This crop, from being an imported article, has of late years become a very large one for export in several of the Southern States. Florida-grown peanuts rank with the best in quantity and quality of production. They are largely used on the farm as food for swine.

PERSIMMON, POMEGRANATE, JAPAN PLUM AND OLIVE.

The persimmon is found wild in every section of the State. The fruit, at least to the natives, is agreeable to the taste, and, ripe or dry, is used largely for the table and for home-made beer.

Pomegranates are of two kinds—the sweet and sour. The bush is large, graceful in foliage, and beautiful in pendant crimson flowers and fruit. As an ornamental tree it is one of the best.

The Japan plum has long been known and grown here. As an ornamental tree it rivals the horse chestnut, which it resembles in size and leaf. The fruit grows in clusters; it is a beautiful creamy white, and has a peculiarly grateful and cool sub-acid taste. It bears shipment well.

With the exception of a few trees, grown for ornament, this most valuable tree, the olive, has not been cultivated in this State. Recently, attention has been directed to its cultivation, and it will become widely planted. It commences to bear at about ten years from the seed, increasing yearly to the age of thirty years, bearing annually.

INDIGO, CASTOR BEAN AND SILK.

The indigo plant is indigenous in Florida; during the English occupation it was extensively cultivated, manufactured and exported; now it is occasionally raised for domestic use. The castor bean here attains the size of a tree often thirty feet high, grows rapidly, and bears largely; now only used for home purposes. Silk some years ago attracted a good deal of attention, but is now only occasionally produced as a pastime. The different species of mulberry grow here to perfection from root, cutting or graft; in leaf from March to October. In time, no doubt, the business will become a regular industry.

SISAL HEMP, RAMIE, JUTE.

All of the fibrous plants grown in warm latitudes are found here. Some years ago the sisal hemp was largely grown, but the Indian war broke up the country where it was planted, and the cultivation has not been resumed. In the many new industries awaiting development, these superior fibrous plants and many others will become prominent.

ARROWROOT, CASSAVA, COMPTIE.

All these grow well when cultivated, and produce astonishingly. Florida arrowroot grades in quality and price with the best Bermuda. Cassava, from which starch and tapioca are made, attains great size. Comptie, the bread-root of the Indians, grows without any cultivation. All the above have only been grown for domestic use for starch and for food, and have limited sale in this and adjoining states. The attention of Northern starch manufacturers has lately been drawn to them, and Governor Sinclair, of New Hampshire, having tested the roots by actual experiments, has introduced a pioneer factory. As either and all of these roots have a larger percentage of starch in them than the Irish potato, and can be grown much cheaper, and manufactured all the year, we may look for a large business in this industry.

MISCELLANEOUS.

Of strictly tropical fruits that are worthy of attention, in addition to those above noticed, may be mentioned the guava, sappadillo, sugar apple, tamarind, alligator pear, pawpaw, plantain, cocoanut, and perhaps the date. All the above we have seen growing luxuriantly in South Florida. The cocoanut is a very tall tree, with fruit ripening the year round.

A very valuable text book, entitled "Gardening in Florida," has lately been issued by Prof. J. N. Whitner, of the State Agricult ral College. It details the best methods for raising every variety of fruit and vegetable in this State, and will be found invaluable to all who desire full information on the subject. The price of the book is $1.50. On receipt of $1.60, to cover cost of book and postage, it will be sent by our Land Commissioner at Jacksonville, Fla.

TROPICAL FRUIT CULTURE.

ORANGE CULTURE.

The subject of orange growing in Florida is one on which we often have inquiries addressed to us, and we therefore give additional facts on the much-debated question of the cost and profit of orange growing, for which the United States Department of Agriculture is authority. From barely nothing, in a commercial sense, at the close of the war, the business has grown to be worth over $3,000,000. Measured by the progress of the past, it is destined to become, in a short time, one of the leading industries of the State. Last year there were exported at least 80,000,000 oranges. The business so far has been very successful, and is daily inviting more capital and enterprise. There are already $15,000,000 invested in orange groves in the State, with a field open for the profitable employment of $100,000,000 more. Lands suitable for growing oranges are in abundance at low prices. Orange groves can be found in almost every part of the State, and on all varieties of soil well drained, the groves numbering each from 10 to 10,000 trees. Hardly a family, outside of the cities, but cultivates a greater or less number of orange trees, and many residing in the cities do the same. Some of the largest groves in the State are owned by persons living in the towns, or non-residents. In some of the counties there were raised as high as from 4,000,000 to 6,000,000.of oranges last year; and narrow-gauge railroads are rapidly being built to afford the southern counties' facilities for shipping their enormous crops to market. Three such roads have been completed within the past few months, and others are projected, while more are under contemplation. Oranges are shipped by these roads to New York in eighty and ninety hours' time. Within the past few years orange culture in Florida has attained great perfection. It has reached that position where it is possible to analyze the cost of production. Abundant evidence exists that can be brought forward to show the value and profit in it. For the investment of capital, results have shown that there is not at present any pursuit, where the tilling of the ground is involved, that will yield larger returns with less fluctuation. It is always pleasant to be able to confirm such statements with facts. An extensive orange grower in Putnam county has kept, from the beginning of his grove, an accurate account of the expenditures and receipts to the close of the thirteenth year, ending in 1879. The number of trees was three hundred. They yielded 442,600 oranges, selling for $7,590, against an expenditure, omitting cost of land, first cost of trees, and interest on the money of $1,950. This gives receipts over expenditures $5,640. This is only one instance, but it is as good as many because it is only one in a very large number. It conclusively demonstrates that orange culture is not at all transitory, nearly all the obstacles in the path of orange culture having been removed. The future of the business is still more promising. Florida oranges are conceded to be superior to all others. In point of numbers, compared to the great quantities consumed, they are few, yet by their greater merit they have come to occupy the foremost place in the market. The genial climate and peculiar soil of Florida, together with the sufficiently warm sun to mature and concentrate the juices without destroying the lively aromatic flavor of the fruit, impart this quality-value nowhere else attainable to such an extent. The field they are yet to occupy is practically illimitable. They are yet to possess our own market, the best in the world. This will be the labor of years, and after a great portion of our orange lands have been brought under cultivation. In 1879 there were 257,000,000 oranges entered at the port of New York from foreign countries. Double the number, at least, were entered at all the other ports, making a grand total of 771,000,000 consumed in and lost on the voyage to this country, in addition to our Florida crop. We cannot predict when the domestic will take the place of the foreign product, but it is inevitable in the course of time. Our inability to supply the demand is the main obstacle. That this will be the ultimate result is clear from another cause, independent, or nearly so, of merit. The liability of loss and damage resulting from uncertainties of a sea voyage, forms an important factor in the conduct of the foreign fruit trade, serving to make it extremely hazardous, a circumstance against which dealers do not have to contend in the shipment of Florida oranges. We have railroads leading to all the great markets of America, and when the fruit is transported by water, all facilities are afforded by perfect and commodious steamers. Orange culture, therefore, may go on indefinitely in Florida, without fear of reaching a general redundance of product. When our own market is occupied, those of Europe and elsewhere will be open to us. The growing desire everywhere for semi-tropical fruits, which the efforts of producers are trying to satisfy, is unlimited, and therefore efforts in orange culture can continue to be put forth until this unlimited and independent desire is met—a goal which, perhaps, never can be reached.

To persons of foresight and capital, who are looking to the future rather than the present for remunerative returns, Florida presents, in her orange pursuits, the most extended as well as the most inviting field. But aside from the question of profit, the culture of oranges presents other practical advantages. It is not only a pleasing but an independent occupation. Its pursuit is no dead-level or monotonous exertion, but one that affords scope for the development of an ingenious mind. As to product, the orange grower is working under conditions of constantly increasing advantages. Young men, sometimes with little or no capital, are starting every year in the business, often away from communities of old and experienced growers, and have succeeded by dint of tact and industry. In point of regular profits; in point of an industrious, frugal and cheerful occupation; in point of a very general desire to become independent; in point of repressive and adverse influences in other pursuits, they have found orange culture in its practical working, the most pleasing occupation. Persons who own orange groves in Florida are entirely well satisfied, as a rule, with their investments. A bearing grove is worth a great deal of money, and to purchase one would require a large cash outlay. In ten years' time groves are usually in full bearing—often in less time—and the inducement to plant one is very great.

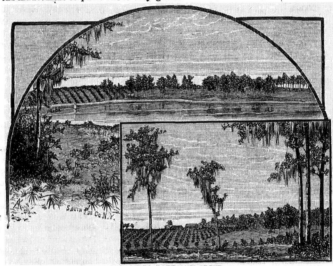

A FLORIDA LAKE AND GROVE.

LEMONS.

The lemon grows well on our sandy soils, and ranks fully equal to the orange in profit. It has the advantage over the orange of coming into bearing sooner. The orange bears in eight to ten years from the seed, while the lemon has fruit in four years. The few fruit growers who have been far sighted enough to plant lemon groves, are now reaping the benefit of their foresight. The fruit is quoted, and actually sells for as much as the orange, and after beginning to bear requires far less care and attention. It is capable of standing nearly as much cold as the orange, but fruits best where the climate is mild.

Experiments have demonstrated that the lemon will not produce its like from the seed, while the orange in most instances will. The lemon should be budded. One of the largest fruit dealers in New York writing on the lemon says: " The best lemons we get here are those from Florida, because, in the first place, they are naturally splendid lemons, and in the second place, the distance they have to come is so short that they arrive in perfect condition. I paid two years ago as high as $12 a box for Florida lemons. They were of extra fine quality, of course, for there were other Florida lemons sold at the same time for $3 and $4 per box, but the fact that they could command such a price is an indication of the possibilities before the lemon growers of Florida. They can practically run out Italy in time if they will only take care in growing, sorting and packing, and send to New York the best lemons. The Florida lemons are packed in boxes holding from 250 to 350 each. They are shipped about November."

One prominent fruit grower of Orange county, about three years ago budded from a fine variety of Sicily lemon. Last winter he shipped 1,000,000 lemons; next year he will market 3,000,000; with an annual increase thereafter. His lemons are picked and shipped after they mature, and command one dollar a box in advance of the finest imported lemons on the market.

LIMES.

There is not a more useful and acceptable fruit grown in the State than the lime. It is produced very successfully on our hammock and pine land in the southern counties, flourishing best where cold weather never visits. It comes to maturity and bears even sooner than the lemon, having fruit in three years from planting the seed. Limes are attracting considerable attention in the Northern market, where they are esteemed superior to the lemon, containing more acid, and being better shippers. Some shipments have proved very remunerative, the fruit selling for 30 cents per dozen in quantity.

The " pickled lime" is regarded as one of the best appetizers and antibilious tonics known. It is prepared as follows: The lime is plucked, when just ripe, a barrel is filled with them and closed up. Through the bung as much ordinary sea water is poured upon them as the barrel will hold, and allowed to remain for twenty-four hours, the water is then poured off and replaced by a fresh supply of sea-water, which is allowed to remain another twenty-four hours and then poured off. Fill the barrel a third time in this way with sea water, close the bung and the limes are then ready for use and shipment as "pickled limes." The lime requires very little cultivation, and is almost entirely exempt from the diseases to which the other members of the citrus family are liable.

CANE.

The soil best adapted to the cultivation of cane is a moist black loam underlaid with clay or marl, large areas of which are found among the prairies owned by these Companies in the Kissimmee and Coloosahatchie Valleys, which are pronounced by experienced sugar raisers from Louisiana and Cuba to be unsurpassed in the world. They have an average depth of three feet of rich vegetable mold, with a subsoil of calcareous marl. The cane is planted continuously in drills six feet apart, and yields its largest crop the subsequent years, but requires replanting every seven years for best results. It lives the year round in this section, and "goes to tassel," as the saying is, every year, reaching a length of seventeen feet in a season.

To those who have watched the development of the resources of Florida, it is apparent that sugar is the "king" field product of the State, and with the developments now making it will be but a comparatively short period until a large percentage of the sugar and molasses consumed in the United States will be drawn from the rich soils of the Peninsular State. Of all the districts in the Union adapted to the cultivation of sugar cane, no region is so favored in soil and climate as Florida—the soil of the rich bottom lands being admirably fitted to the maturing of cane crops. It is no extravagant statement to say that many hundreds of thousands of acres are here awaiting development. Sugar cane is grown on the pine lands with good results, where a little attention is given to cow-penning or fertilizing. The climatic conditions are most favorable in South Florida for the production of the crop; no danger is to be apprehended from frost, which in these latitudes has never been known to injure the cane crop. Here the cane matures and perfects its seed, even when grown for years on the same land without manure. It is customary to replant sugar cane every two or three years in the more northern sugar belts of the country. Sugar cane readily responds to frequent cultivation and fertilization, however, in the southern portion of this State. It is no uncommon circumstance to see good stands of cane that have rattooned more than ten years. On the shores of Lake Worth cane was recently seen growing that had not been replanted since the Seminole wars.

The cost of fencing, plowing and planting the first cane crop upon these prairie lands averages about fifty dollars per acre. The soil is inexhaustible, and needs no fertilizer. The net profits the second year easily amount to eighty dollars per acre, and many growers realize much higher profits.

COCOANUTS.

The entire coast line of Monroe county will in a few years become a vast cocoanut grove, both climate and soil being specially adapted to their growth. The prevailing type of country is a low sandy plain or prairie, where the cocoanut is found to grow and thrive luxuriantly, little or no care being required beyond the original planting. Single, scattered trees are to be found all along the coast, where they appear to have sprung spontaneously from the seed nuts which have been washed ashore. Trees are found on the Keys, at Cape Sable and among the islands in Charlotte Harbor, in fact all along the coast range for three hundred miles.

Bearing groves are found throughout the county. Groves are now bearing upon and near Key West island, at Plantation Key in the reef range, and at Charlotte Harbor. Major Evans has a grove in his garden at Myers, upon the Caloosahatchie, which produces 300 or more nuts per tree annually. He gathers bunches of twenty, twenty-five and even thirty-four nuts each, and trees are blooming and bearing all the year round, and this seems to be the average production of fully developed trees in South Florida.

It is but recently that this industry has received much attention. The cultivation of cocoanuts, like that of pine-apples, is still in its infancy here, but astonishing figures can be shown, considering the brief time which has elapsed since its commencement. Captain Henry Geiger was the pioneer, and his grove at Boca Chica, near Key West, is now bearing—the interest of farmers and enterprising capitalists was soon attracted to this industry, and during the past few years all the available lands in this immediate vicinity have been secured and planted, and the work is still progressing and extending to the mainland with marvelous rapidity. Three hundred and twenty-five thousand trees are now planted and growing within the limits of Monroe county, of which fifty thousand were set out last year. These are mostly upon the line of keys from Cape Florida to Key West. Cocoanut planting became a "boom" and soon reached the Gulf coast, where extensive groves have been planted at Horsman's Key, Caximbas, Horr's Island, Marco, Myers and Charlotte Harbor, and are all doing well, exceeding even the sanguine hopes of their proprietors.

To show the general feeling and future prospect, one gentleman has purchased a tract of land at Caximbas, and contracted for 30,000 seed-nuts; and at the present moment a vessel has just arrived in Key West harbor, with a cargo of 120,000 nuts, to be planted at Biscayne by a colony recently started. This is but an installment, as they are even now negotiating for 30,000 more nuts, and will in all probability not stop short of 200,000 trees. Others are planting largely along the lower Caloosahatchie Valley with a view to equally large transactions, and it is a question of but a very short time when the desolate monotony of these silent and hitherto practically unknown shores will be supplanted by the tropical beauty and magnificence of an almost continuous cocoanut grove. Nature has done her part and is quietly waiting, and human energy and capital are alone needed for the long-time wilderness to spring into active and profitable life. The annual profit on a cocoanut grove may be safely reckoned at $2 per tree, and one hundred trees to the acre. The trees come into bearing at from six to eight years of age.

It is admitted by all experienced growers that the cocoanut does best on a moist, sandy soil near salt water, but they can be raised on land removed from the coast, if salt is applied to the ground around the trees after they become three years old.

They should be planted as follows : Place the ripe nuts about four inches under the soil, and about twenty feet apart. Care should be taken to plant the nut with the end that is attached to the stem downward, as the milk inside of the nut will then cover the eye and germinate the young sprout that produces the tree.

The tree should make its appearance above ground in from six months to one year after planting the seed.

THE BANANA.

The banana is not properly a tree, but a plant of leafy, succulent growth, of the genus *Musa*. The stock is formed of the stems of the leaves in concentric layers, reaching with its leaves, a height of fifteen or twenty feet, and eight to ten inches in thickness, and contains no woody fibre. From the center comes the first bearing stem, which turns and grows downward. The end has the appearance of an ear of corn with purple shuck. This unfolds one leaf at a time, displaying two rows—eight to twelve each—of tiny, little fruit, with their delicate blossoms, until it attains a length of two or three feet, covered with fruit. The leaves are a marvel for size and appearance, sometimes reaching a length of six feet, and eighteen inches in width, of a glossy pea green. The root is perennial. It is large and fleshy, sometimes of the size of a bushel measure, from which put forth numerous rootlets, half an inch in diameter. From the main root are constantly springing numerous suckers, which go to form new plants. This being its mode of propagation, these suckers can be taken off to form a new plantation, or remain, as may be wanted.

There are several varieties of banana, among which is the dwarf. This plant rarely attains a height of more than seven feet, is readily cultivated in the southern portion of the State, but is too delicate to be safely propagated in the upper tier of counties. The fruit is noted for its large size and delicate flavor and is in demand. At Lake Worth a plantation of bananas has been successfully cultivated for years.

In a suitable soil, which should be rich and moist, and in a tropical climate, it requires about one year to mature fruit, from the first appearance of the plant. Each stock bears but one bunch of fruit. When it is gathered, the stock is cut down. Ten feet apart is a good distance to plant them. This gives over 400 per acre, and the second year there will be six or eight plants to each hill, and soon occupy most of the ground. After the first year they require but little cultivation, the old stalk and leaves acting as mulch and manure. Under favorable conditions there is no cessation of growth. New plants and ripe fruit are found at all times, and a plantation once started lasts for years.

It is probable that no fruit was ever cultivated that will yield more fruit per acre, or result in greater profit to the owner, where there is a market for it. It is easily and cheaply gathered, requiring no packages, and bears handling and transportation well. Three bunches a year per hill is a fair estimate for the yield of a good plantation. This would give over 1,200 bunches per acre. Many of these will contain over 100 bananas each. It is a favorite food in tropical countries, and always in demand at the seaport towns for shipment. There are some people, no doubt, who live on bananas alone; but it is not probable that any amount of work can be got out of a dozen of that fruit a day. Southern Florida and some of the islands on its coast have proved to be suitable and profitable for the culture of the banana, and instances are mentioned where the receipts have been over $3,000 per year from a single acre, including plants sold.

PINE-APPLE.

The cultivation of this most delicious fruit is becoming one of the leading industries of South Florida.

Fully 800 acres are now under cultivation in Monroe county, and the area is being constantly increased as fast as the land can be cleared and the slips can be produced from which they are propagated. The area devoted to this business in Monroe is confined principally to Key Largo and the adjacent keys, where the enterprise was originally started, but the farmers in Manatee and the mainland of Monroe are now turning their attention to this industry, and large fields have been planted in several of the southern counties. Those already started are reported in excellent condition, and the outlook for rapid increase is exceedingly promising. We cite a few figures which have been obtained from accurate information about Key Largo and vicinity. The shipments of pine-apples to Northern markets have been about as follows: In 1881, 30,000 dozen; in 1882, 75,000 dozen, and in 1883, 150,000 dozen. An acre of land set out in pine slips will produce 8,000 pine-apples, the average price of which, when ready for shipping, is $5 per hundred. The Largo pines are already well known, and those which have been produced upon the mainland demonstrate fully that the pine lands of South Florida are well adapted to the production of strong, healthy plants, and a sweet, fine quality of fruit.

. The pine-apple is propagated from slips and suckers; the former are taken from the base of the matured pine-apple—each pine producing from five to seven slips. The suckers grow up from the root of the plant, and after being removed and dried, stand shipment very well. An excess of moisture in slips and suckers when shipped in quantity is detrimental; in this condition they are liable to deteriorate. After planting, the slips will produce fruit in from eighteen months to two years. The suckers fruit in one year under favorable conditions. Pine-apples require but little attention; their luxuriant growth soon shades the ground, preventing the growth of weeds and rapid evaporation of moisture.

Experienced growers express themselves fully satisfied with their present success, and are going into the business largely.

RICE.

Both the lowland and upland varieties of this most useful grain are grown successfully and profitably in "lorida. On the rich hammock lands of the interior of the State, and the ." pine lands of the South, upland rice of the best quality is raised by small planters, while the rich valleys of the Kissim-mee and Caloosahatchie will produce wonderful yields of the lowland and this, too, without the irrigation which is regarded so essential to its produc-tion in Georgia and South Carolina. It requires a moist soil, is sown in drills, and when kept clear of weeds will produce thirty to 100 bushels of rough rice to the acre. Rice is a standard article of food and is used in many manufac-turing processes, and there is certainly no reason why its culture should not become at an early day one of the leading industries of this our "State of marvelous resources."

GUAVAS.

Guavas are grown all over South Florida with little cultivation, and are the peaches of that section. For jellies, jams, pies, and to serve with cream, they are the most delicious fruit that grows. When cooked, or prepared in any of the ways in which we serve peaches at table, one soon grows fond of them, and many people relish them eaten from the bush. In addition to its delicious flavor, the guava is a very healthy fruit.

Little attention is given to the manufacture of "guava jelly," though it is confidently believed that it could be made immensely profitable in the southern counties, as the jelly is highly esteemed the world over. When cold-storage warehouses and refrigerator-cars have been introduced, so that the guava can be sent to Northern markets, the demand will be very great.

SUGAR-APPLE.

This fruit grows on a shrub similar to the guava, and is also very tender and needs some protection from cold. The fruit is a rich, yellowish green, and rough on the outside, but it is very rich and sweet, and while it is *sui generis*, it may be compared to a date in taste. This fruit does well south of latitude 28 degrees.

THE MANGO

is a rich and deliciously flavored fruit, larger than an egg, and nearly the same shape. It is a greenish yellow on the outside, and a bright yellow on the inside; the pulp being somewhat fibrous or stringy; it is best to pare and eat with a very sharp knife. It has a large, oblong, single seed, that is quite a curiosity itself. There are several varieties, some of which are hardier than others and more prolific. It is said that the Persian, or East India variety, is most desirable for this State. They are at home on the sandy soils of South Florida, where they come into bearing in five years from planting the seed. The trees resemble the orange tree in size and shape. They produce about 2,000 mangoes each, which are principally sold in Southern markets, and bring from $1 to $3 per hundred.

THE AVOCADO PEAR,

usually called "alligator pear," is a peculiar fruit, native to the West Indies. The fruit is very large, pear-shaped, and has a large, round kernel or seed, in the center. The fruit, even when mature, is a dark green, sometimes shaded yellow, and the flesh is of the same color. The taste is peculiarly oily and pasty, and one must be educated to a relish for it. It is generally eaten with salt, vinegar and pepper; as a salad, it is highly esteemed. The tree is a model of beauty, and grows to a large size on the shell hammocks and sandy soils of South Florida. It commences bearing in five years from the seed. Will produce from 200 to 300 pears when eight years old, which are readily sold in Key West market at prices ranging from 60 cents to $1.20 per dozen.

The mango and alligator pear are growing and maturing their fruit at Point Pinellas, a peculiarly favored spot just west of Tampa Bay. This point, due to the water protection afforded by the waters of the Gulf, Hillsborough Bay and Tampa Bay, is as tropical in its conditions as points on the mainland one hundred and thirty miles further south, and presents unusual attractions to those desiring an equable climate or a point for tropical fruit and early vegetable cultivation. Shaddocks, grape-fruit, sapadillos, sour-sops, Jamaica apples, pawpaws and dates are all grown to some extent in the southern counties, but there are not enough raised to create a demand in the market.

VEGETABLE GROWING.

In the southern portion of the State, tomatoes, green peas, cucumbers, egg-plant, new potatoes, strawberries, watermelons, etc., may be seen growing side by side and in the same field in the month of December. The completion of new lines of railroad now building, in connection with water transportation, will afford facilities for placing these desirable garden products on the Northern table at a season when there will be no competition, and prices obtained will return a large profit.

CASAVA AND COMPTIE.

Starch and glucose can be more easily and profitably made from the casava and comptie than from any other plants known. But as the comptie could not be so easily, abundantly and profitably raised as the

CASAVA,

the latter would be the general crop. It produces more in weight and bulk to a given area than any other of the root family, often reaching, as we are reliably informed, forty tons to the acre; and this in turn yields a larger percentage of merchantable product than any of the bulbous plants, about 30 per cent. of glucose or syrup, 40 per cent. of starch, and 10 per cent. of the residuum tapioca, there being no waste but the thin rind.

As a stock for the manufacture of starch, casava, in cheapness of production and yield per acre, is superior to any other field crop, with the added advantage that the tubers may remain in the ground after maturing and increase in weight very rapidly. About three thousand plants are set to the acre, and it is no unusual circumstance to find roots of thirty to sixty pounds each. The crop may be gathered eight months after planting. There are several million of acres of land strictly adapted to this crop under our control. A company is now planting on the Gulf coast for the purpose of manufacture of glucose.

STOCK RAISING.

It is quite difficult, in the limits of a publication of this character, to discuss the best methods of stock raising.

In all the Southern counties are to be found large and small herds of cattle. These run at large through the pine woods, swamps and vast prairies of the Kissimmee and Caloosahatchie valleys, and thrive on the coarse pasturage in a manner quite remarkable and satisfactory to their owners, who "round-up" once a year, mark and brand the young calves, and give little other attention to them.

So little expense attends this sort of stock raising that notwithstanding the small size of the cattle produced, they prove most profitable for shipment to the Cuban markets. Indeed, the hide and tallow of a five-year-old steer would return a good profit on the cost of his keeping. The cattle are not so large as those grown in Texas, because less attention has been given here to improving the native breeds of stock. The cattle raised in Florida are small, with thick, heavy necks and fore parts and narrow loins; but when fat a four-year-old when dressed will weigh from 400 to 500 pounds.

The buyers in the Cuban markets (to which shipments are made to the extent of 50,000 head per year), prefer Florida to Texas beef. The grasses in the southern counties are more nutritious, and seem to impart a more agreeable flavor to the flesh than in the northern part of Florida. That this business pays well has this practical proof: More money has been made in stock raising in South Florida than any other enterprise in the State until quite recently, and a number have thus grown wealthy from their herds. The improving of our breeds of cattle and proper experiments with the grasses which may be grown successfully here, will make stock raising in Florida as general as it is profitable, and will give a value to a vast area in the State now practically a wilderness.

To enumerate in detail the varied crops and products of this country would be beyond the province of this paper. Crops indigenous to all parts of America may be safely grown (excepting in the case of a few of the cereals) with less care and labor in their cultivation and production; besides, in many cases the soil can be replanted the same year. The region represented by our Companies presents the advantage of a tropical and semi-tropical climate. It is the region where many of the products of both the temperate and tropical climes may be found growing side by side—where the orange, lemon, lime, guava, fig, etc., and all the garden vegetables may be grown for profit in the open air the year round. It is where cotton, sugar-cane, rice, tobacco and all Southern field crops pay best.

Large orange groves are being set out yearly, and the production from those in bearing returns handsome incomes to their owners. In this region frost rarely comes, and every fruit, flower, shrub, plant or product that grows in any semi-tropical or tropical region of the world matures or can be produced. Here one may behold trees in rapid and perennial growth, forests and fields spread with a rich vegetation, and roses in full bloom at a period when the Northern States are wrapped in snow.

This is the region in which to seek the benefits of a summer climate during the winter months. Although the winters are so mild, the summers do not bring the tropical heat which might be expected, and parties now permanently residing here, after several years' experience, assert that they do not suffer more in summer than they did in their old homes in the North. Any person accustomed to exposure, North or South, can do ordinary farm work during the summer without fear of ill effect from the heat. The thermometer rarely rises above ninety degrees.

Official records show the average temperature of Florida to be: summer, seventy-eight; winter, sixty degrees.

The daily ocean breezes in summer modify the heat. The Gulf breeze coming in with the setting sun cools the air at night.

Official sanitary reports, both of scientific bodies and the army, show that Florida stands first in health, although in the reports are included a transient population, many of whom take refuge here as invalids in the lowest stage of disease.

The flow of immigration already so great to the "Far West" is settling in upon these lands, so much more advantageously located for marketing products, and possessing superior adaptability to the profitable pursuit of a pleasing agriculture.

The influx of population will rapidly advance the price of these lands in the hands of the husbandman, and the great variety of adaptation and products, with a ready access to the best markets of the world, will certainly work a large and more certain return for labor and capital than in the frigid regions of the more Northern States.

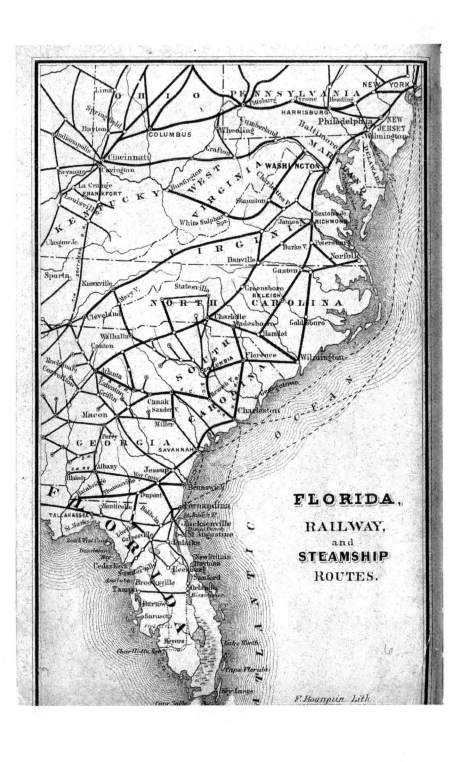

FLORIDA,
RAILWAY,
and
STEAMSHIP
ROUTES.

CPSIA information can be obtained
at www.ICGtesting.com
Printed in the USA
BVHW031015010722
641096BV00010B/838

9 781013 876295